A Literature Kit™ FOR

Sarah, Plain and Tall

● ● ● ● ● ● ● ● ● ● ● ● ● ● ● ●

By Patricia MacLachlan

Written by Nat Reed

GRADES 3 - 4

Classroom Complete Press

P.O. Box 19729
San Diego, CA 92159
Tel: 1-800-663-3609 / Fax: 1-800-663-3608
Email: service@classroomcompletepress.com

www.classroomcompletepress.com

ISBN-13: 978-1-55319-446-0
ISBN-10: 1-55319-446-2

© 2009

Critical Thinking Skills

Sarah, Plain and Tall

Skills For Critical Thinking		Ch 1	Ch 2	Ch 3	Ch 4	Ch 5	Ch 6	Ch 7	Ch 8	Ch 9	Review	Writing Tasks	Graphic Organizers
LEVEL 1 Remembering	• Identify Story Elements	✓	✓	✓	✓	✓	✓	✓	✓	✓	✓	✓	✓
	• Recall Details	✓	✓	✓	✓	✓	✓	✓	✓	✓	✓	✓	✓
	• Match	✓	✓	✓	✓	✓	✓	✓	✓	✓	✓		
	• Sequence Events		✓			✓						✓	✓
LEVEL 2 Understanding	• Compare and Contrast	✓				✓	✓	✓		✓	✓	✓	✓
	• Summarize	✓	✓	✓	✓	✓	✓	✓	✓	✓	✓	✓	✓
	• State Main Idea				✓		✓	✓	✓	✓	✓	✓	✓
	• Describe	✓	✓	✓	✓	✓	✓	✓	✓	✓	✓	✓	✓
	• Classify					✓		✓	✓		✓		✓
LEVEL 3 Applying	• Plan	✓	✓	✓	✓	✓	✓	✓	✓	✓	✓	✓	✓
	• Interview											✓	
	• Infer Outcomes		✓	✓	✓	✓	✓	✓	✓	✓	✓		✓
LEVEL 4 Analysing	• Draw Conclusions	✓	✓	✓	✓	✓	✓	✓	✓	✓	✓	✓	✓
	• Identify Supporting Evidence	✓		✓	✓	✓	✓		✓	✓	✓		✓
	• Motivations	✓	✓	✓	✓								✓
	• Identify Cause and Effect	✓		✓		✓	✓	✓	✓	✓	✓		✓
LEVEL 5 Evaluating	• State & Defend An Opinion	✓	✓	✓	✓	✓	✓	✓	✓	✓	✓	✓	✓
	• Make Judgements	✓	✓	✓	✓	✓	✓	✓	✓	✓	✓	✓	✓
LEVEL 6 Creating	• Predict	✓	✓	✓		✓	✓	✓	✓	✓	✓		✓
	• Design											✓	✓
	• Create	✓			✓							✓	✓
	• Imagine Alternatives		✓			✓	✓	✓	✓	✓	✓	✓	✓

Based on Bloom's Taxonomy

2

Contents

🍎 TEACHER GUIDE

- Assessment Rubric 4
- How is Our Literature Kit™ Organized? 5
- Graphic Organizers 6
- Bloom's Taxonomy for Reading Comprehension 7
- Teaching Strategies 7
- Summary of the Story.. 8
- Vocabulary 9

✏️ STUDENT HANDOUTS

- Spotlight on Patricia MacLachlan.................................... 10
- Chapter Questions
  - *Chapter 1* 11
  - *Chapter 2* 14
  - *Chapter 3* 17
  - *Chapter 4* 20
  - *Chapter 5* 23
  - *Chapter 6* 26
  - *Chapter 7* 29
  - *Chapter 8* 32
  - *Chapter 9* 35
  - *Review* 38
- Writing Tasks 41
- Word Search... 44
- Comprehension Quiz 45

EZ✔ EASY MARKING™ ANSWER KEY 47

GRAPHIC ORGANIZERS 53

✔ **6 BONUS Activity Pages!** Additional worksheets for your students

FREE!

- Go to our website: **www.classroomcompletepress.com/bonus**
- Enter item CC2308 – Sarah, Plain and Tall
- Enter pass code CC2308D for Activity Pages

Assessment Rubric

• • • • • • • • • • • • • • • • • •

Sarah, Plain and Tall

Student's Name: _____   Assignment: _____   Level: _____

Criteria	Level 1	Level 2	Level 3	Level 4
Comprehension of Novel	Demonstrates a limited understanding of the novel	Demonstrates a basic understanding of the novel	Demonstrates a good understanding of the novel	Demonstrates a thorough understanding of the novel
Content • Information and details relevant to focus	Elements incomplete; key details missing	Some elements complete; details missing	All required elements completed; key details contain some description	All required elements completed; enough description for clarity
Style • Effective word choice and originality • Precise language	Little variety in word choice. Language vague and imprecise	Some variety in word choice. Language somewhat vague and imprecise	Good variety in word choice. Language precise and quite descriptive	Writer's voice is apparent throughout. Excellent choice of words. Precise language
Conventions • Spelling, language, capitalization, punctuation	Errors seriously interfere with the writer's purpose	Repeated errors in mechanics and usage	Some errors in convention	Few errors in convention

STRENGTHS:

WEAKNESSES:

NEXT STEPS:

Sarah, Plain and Tall CC2308

Teacher Guide

Our resource has been created for ease of use by both TEACHERS and STUDENTS alike.

Introduction

This study guide is designed to give the teacher a number of helpful ways to make the study of this novel a more enjoyable and profitable experience for the students. The guide features a number of useful and flexible components, from which the teacher can choose. It is not expected that all of the activities will be completed.

One advantage of this approach to the study of a novel is that the student can work at his/her own speed, and the teacher can assign activities, which match the student's abilities.

The study guide generally divides the novel by chapter and features reading comprehension and vocabulary questions. Themes include the importance of home and family, perseverance, loyalty, loneliness, adapting to new circumstances, loss and death. **Sarah, Plain and Tall** provides a wealth of opportunity for classroom discussion because of its vivid portrayal of the central characters – especially the challenges faced by the two Witting children with the arrival of Sarah, their father's "mail-order bride".

How Is Our Literature Kit™ Organized?

STUDENT HANDOUTS

Chapter Activities (in the form of reproducible worksheets) make up the majority of this resource. For each chapter or group of chapters there are BEFORE YOU READ activities and AFTER YOU READ activities.

- The BEFORE YOU READ activities prepare students for reading by setting a purpose for reading. They stimulate background knowledge and experience, and guide students to make connections between what they know and what they will learn. Important concepts and vocabulary from the chapter(s) are also presented.

- The AFTER YOU READ activities check students' comprehension and extend their learning. Students are asked to give thoughtful consideration of the text through creative and evaluative short-answer questions and journal prompts.

Six **Writing Tasks** and three **Graphic Organizers** are included to further develop students' critical thinking and writing skills, and analysis of the text. *(See page 6 for suggestions on using the Graphic Organizers.)* The **Assessment Rubric** *(page 4)* is a useful tool for evaluating students' responses to the Writing Tasks and Graphic Organizers.

PICTURE CUES

This resource contains three main types of pages, each with a different purpose and use. A **Picture Cue** at the top of each page shows, at a glance, what the page is for.

Teacher Guide
- Information and tools for the teacher

Student Handout
- Reproducible worksheets and activities

Easy Marking™ Answer Key
- Answers for student activities

EASY MARKING™ ANSWER KEY

Marking students' worksheets is fast and easy with this **Answer Key**. Answers are listed in columns – just line up the column with its corresponding worksheet, as shown, and see how every question matches up with its answer!

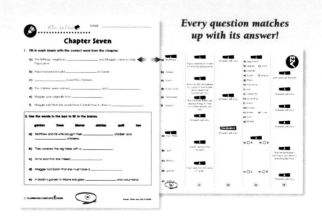

Every question matches up with its answer!

1,2,3
Graphic Organizers

The three **Graphic Organizers** included in this Literature Kit™ are especially suited to a study of **Sarah, Plain and Tall**. Below are suggestions for using each organizer in your classroom. They could also may be adapted to suit the individual needs of your students. The organizers can be used on a projection system or interactive whiteboard in teacher-led activities, and/or photocopied for use as student worksheets. To evaluate students' responses to any of the organizers, you may wish to use the **Assessment Rubric** (on page 4).

COMPARISON CHART

Sarah's former home in Maine was quite different from her new home on the prairies with the Witting family. In the **Comparison Chart** students are asked to consider five things which are similar between the two homes, and five things that are different. The details of these choices then are listed under the second and third columns. It would probably be profitable for the teacher to lead the class in a brainstorming session before attempting the activity. Found on Page 53.

MAKING UP SARAH'S MIND

It must have been difficult for Sarah to decide whether or not to stay with the Wittings. She came as a complete stranger, and within one short month was expected to decide her future for the rest of her life. Students are asked to imagine that they are in Sarah's position, and using the chart provided, they are to list as many reasons both for staying and leaving as they can think of. They are then asked to select one or two of the reasons from each category which they feel are the most convincing for staying or leaving. Found on Page 54.

SEQUENCE CHART

The plot of **Sarah, Plain and Tall** is filled with memorable events – so much so that it is a tall order to isolate the "main events" of the novel, as this assignment expects. In assigning the **Sequence Chart** activity, it might be helpful for the teacher to remind the students that each event selected should be a key component in moving the plot toward the climax of the novel (the scene where Sarah returns to the farm after her trip to town). Found on Page 55.

Bloom's Taxonomy* for Reading Comprehension

The activities in this resource engage and build the full range of thinking skills that are essential for students' reading comprehension. Based on the six levels of thinking in Bloom's Taxonomy, questions are given that challenge students to not only recall what they have read, but to move beyond this to understand the text through higher-order thinking. By using higher-order skills of applying, analysing, evaluating and creating, students become active readers, drawing more meaning from the text, and applying and extending their learning in more sophisticated ways.

This Literature Kit™, therefore, is an effective tool for any Language Arts program. Whether it is used in whole or in part, or adapted to meet individual student needs, this resource provides teachers with the important questions to ask, inspiring students' interest, creativity, and promoting meaningful learning.

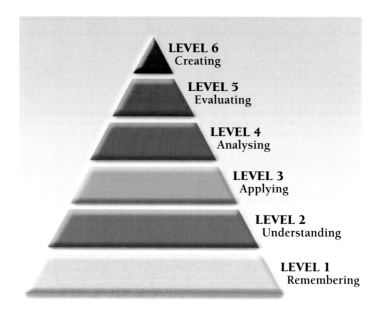

LEVEL 6 Creating
LEVEL 5 Evaluating
LEVEL 4 Analysing
LEVEL 3 Applying
LEVEL 2 Understanding
LEVEL 1 Remembering

BLOOM'S TAXONOMY: 6 LEVELS OF THINKING

Bloom's Taxonomy is a tool widely used by educators for classifying learning objectives, and is based on the work of Benjamin Bloom.

Teaching Strategies — INDEPENDENT, SMALL GROUP OR WHOLE CLASS STUDY

This study guide contains the following activities:

Before Reading Activities: themes are introduced and thought-provoking questions put forward for the students to consider.

Vocabulary Activities: new and unfamiliar words are introduced and reviewed.

After Reading Questions: the first part of this section includes short answer questions dealing with the content of the play. The second part features questions that are more open-ended and feature concepts from the higher order of Bloom's Taxonomy.

Writing Tasks: creative writing assignments based on Bloom's Taxonomy that relate to the plot of the particular scenes

A **comprehension quiz** is also included comprised of short-answer questions.

Graphic Organizers: three full-page reproducible sheets. One has been designed as an alternative to the traditional book report.

Bonus Sheets are also available online.

The study guide can be used in a variety of ways in the classroom depending on the needs of the students and teacher. The teacher may choose to use an independent reading approach with students capable of working independently. It also works well with small groups, with most of the lessons being quite easy to follow. Finally, in other situations, teachers will choose to use it with their entire class.

Teachers may wish to have their students keep a daily reading log so that they might record their daily progress and reflections.

Summary of the Story

Jacob Witting, a Kansas farmer living in the late 1800s, has been raising his two children, Anna and Caleb, alone since their mother died when Caleb was born. When he comes to realize it is more than he can handle, he advertises for a wife in an eastern newspaper. A young woman from Maine, Sarah Wheaton, answers and agrees to come and stay with the family for a month, to see if things are to her liking.

Sarah, it turns out, is a woman of independent mind and spirit. She wears overalls and is determined to do her share of the work around the farm. She learns how to ride a horse, drive a wagon, help with the plowing, and even assists Jacob when the roof needs repair. The children and Jacob quickly grow to love her, but as it becomes evident that Sarah misses her home and the sea, they are deathly afraid she will decide to return to her home in Maine.

When Sarah decides one day to take the wagon to town by herself, both Anna and Caleb fear that she will catch the train to the east and they will never see her again. Sarah, however, does return, and the children finally realize that there will indeed be a summer wedding in the Witting household.

List of Resources

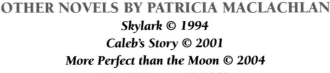

OTHER NOVELS BY PATRICIA MACLACHLAN
Skylark © 1994
Caleb's Story © 2001
More Perfect than the Moon © 2004
Cassie Binegar © 1982
Grandfather's Dance © 2006

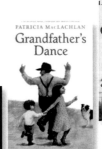

OTHER RECOMMENDED RESOURCES
Laura Ingalls Wilder, Little House on the Prairie © 1935
Heather Collins, A Pioneer Story: The Daily Life of a Canadian Family in 1840 © 1994
Louise Erdrich, The Birchbark House © 1999
Marissa Moss, Rachel's Journal: The Story of a Pioneer Girl © 1998
Jean Van Leeuwen and Rebbeca Bond, Papa and the Pioneer Quilt © 2007
Andrea Warren, Pioneer Girl: Growing up on the Prairie © 2000

List of Vocabulary

CHAPTER 1
• dusk • homely • feisty • harsh • insult • troublesome • familiar • wretched • colt • advertisement • stroked • teakettle • housekeeper • neighbor • hearthstones • prairie • seriously • dough • lap • energetic

CHAPTER 2
• flounder • pesky • prefer • braid • pitchfork • stall • damp • enclose • amaze • grin • bonnet • shingle • bass • bluefish • fog-bound • truly • footprints • nearby • neighbors • bedding

CHAPTER 3
• suspend • woodchuck • chores • alarm • clattered • preacher • quilt • windmill • hitched • paintbrush • wagon • shoveled • marble • Russian • olive • snail • smoothest • whispered • perfect • curled

CHAPTER 4
• roamer • windowsill • scallop • oyster • razor • clam • conch • prairie • violets • clover • asters • ceiling • whisper • ragwort • woolly • velvet • rustle • meadowlark • insects • collection

CHAPTER 5
• crept • coarse • mound • canvas • dunes • meadow • exclaimed • favorite • buzzards • spruce • cliffs • windmill • porch • mica • rotting • wooden • fireflies • sneezed • rotting • charcoal

CHAPTER 6
• sharply • chant • collapse • sleeve • gully • tread • gleam • tumbleweed • killdeer • stiff • chores • sums • frowned • sparkling • biscuits • sweaters • duckling • golden • petticoat • guiding

CHAPTER 7
• primly • shuffled • hitch • marigolds • greens • tansy • dandelions • porch • braids • whickering • banty • quilt • dough • Tennessee • zinnias • blanket • dahlias • columbine • nasturtiums • violet

CHAPTER 8
• argument • crisply • overalls • wisps • portion • pungent • squall • weary • eerie • nipped • marbles • stubbornly • carpenter • horribly • flattened • huddled • trembling • crackling • dawn • bundles

CHAPTER 9
• complained • stern • wailed • dusk • damaged • groom • hailstones • replanted • sly • hush • scuttling • echoing • bundle • murmured • whisper • pesky • wearily • squinted • shovel • nasturtium

Patricia MacLachlan

Patricia MacLachlan was born in Cheyene, Wyoming in 1938.

She is a best selling children's author who achieved fame for winning the Newbery Medal in 1986 for her novel, *Sarah, Plain and Tall.*

As a child, Patricia loved music and loved to read. Her favorite books included **Child's Garden of Verses, Ferdinand,** and every single dog book she could get her hands on.

Sarah, Plain and Tall came from a "real life" connection. The Sarah in "real life" was in fact Patricia's great grandmother. Although she didn't intend for there to be sequels to this famous novel, Patricia became fascinated with the characters of the novel, and continued their stories in two additional books, *Skylark* and *Caleb's Story.* About the characters of this trilogy Patricia says: *I relate to all the characters: I like Jacob because he is, in the end, brave and caring. I like Sarah because she is wise. I like Caleb's directness and his poignant need for everything to work well in the family.*

Surprisingly, Patricia didn't begin to write until she was 35 years old – after her three children were all in school. Her first book was published in 1977.

After spending a few years in Minnesota, she traveled to the East Coast to attend the University of Connecticut. She married psychologist Robert MacLachlan and had three children. From the very beginning, her family has always come before anything else.

She has been the recipient of many awards including the **National Humanities Medal.**

Did You Know..?

- **Patricia lives on a mountain in Western Massachusetts with her husband, Bob.**

- **The book Sarah Plain and Tall was turned into a TV movie starring Glenn Close.**

- **Patricia was an only child. Her lack of siblings was offset by a strong relationship with her parents and an active imagination.**

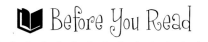

Chapter One

1. What two things do you think would be most **difficult** about living as a pioneer on the American prairies a hundred years ago?

_____

_____

_____

2. What two things do you think would be **fun** about living as a pioneer on the American prairies a hundred years ago?

_____

_____

_____

Vocabulary

Choose a word from the list that means the same or nearly the same as the underlined word.

harsh	wretched	colt	advertisement	dusk
familiar	troublesome	homely	feisty	insult

1. At <u>twilight</u> the family all gathered on the porch to relax and enjoy each other's company.

_____

2. Everyone assumed that she was going to be <u>unattractive</u>. _____

3. The horse, Jack, was the most <u>spirited</u> animal Sarah had ever seen. _____

4. My aunt spoke in a <u>severe</u> tone to the three small children playing in her yard. _____

5. I didn't mean to <u>slight</u> you by saying that you weren't very ambitious. _____

6. When Caleb was born, Anna found him to be very <u>upsetting</u>. _____

7. The two brothers were very <u>close</u> to everyone on their street. _____

8. Never had Anna seen such a <u>pathetic</u> looking baby before. _____

9. Helen was overjoyed when the <u>baby horse</u> arrived at the ranch. _____

10. They paid a lot to the *Toronto Star* to have them print the full-color <u>promotion</u>. _____

Chapter One

1. Put a check mark (✓) next to the answer that is most correct.

a) How often did Caleb and Anna's mother sing?

- ○ **A**   once or twice a week
- ○ **B**   every day
- ○ **C**   not often
- ○ **D**   never

b) What were the names of the two dogs?

- ○ **A**   Tom and Jerry
- ○ **B**   Joe and Snoopy
- ○ **C**   Lottie and Nick
- ○ **D**   Spot and Pumpkin

c) When Caleb was born, Anna <u>really</u> thought he was:

- ○ **A**   beautiful
- ○ **B**   homely, plain and smelly
- ○ **C**   very talented for a baby
- ○ **D**   well-mannered

d) How long did it take Anna to love Caleb?

- ○ **A**   almost a year
- ○ **B**   two weeks
- ○ **C**   three months
- ○ **D**   three days

e) What two things did their mother sing about?

- ○ **A**   flowers and birds
- ○ **B**   sunshine and lollipops
- ○ **C**   animals and children
- ○ **D**   the sea and the sky

Chapter One

Answer each question with a complete sentence or short paragraph.

1. Why do you think Caleb was interested in knowing whether or not his dad and mom sang?

_____

_____

2. Why do you think Caleb and Anna's father didn't sing anymore?

_____

_____

3. According to Anna, what was the worst thing about Caleb?

_____

_____

4. Why had Papa placed an advertisement in the newspaper?

_____

_____

5. Why do you think that Papa waited until he received an answer from Sarah before he told the children he had written to her?

_____

_____

6. What question did Anna suggest her dad ask Sarah in his next letter? Why do you think she suggested this?

_____

_____

Journaling Prompt

Imagine you are Anna. Make an entry in your journal about the day of your mother's death. Describe your innermost feelings at the loss of your mother – and the arrival of your new brother.

NAME: _____

Chapter Two

1. What might be difficult about being a *mail order bride*?

_____

_____

2. How might the arrival of a mail order bride be difficult for a family with children?

_____

_____

Vocabulary

With a straight line, connect each word on the left with its meaning on the right.

1	flounder		a hair style
2	pesky		a compartment in a stable
3	prefer		a type of fish
4	braid		smile
5	pitchfork		choose
6	stall		roof covering
7	damp		farm instrument
8	enclose		a woman's hat
9	amaze		overwhelm with surprise
10	grin		annoying
11	bonnet		moist
12	shingle		surround

Chapter Two

1. (Circle) **T** if the statement is TRUE or **F** if it is FALSE.

T   F   a)   In her letter to Anna, Sarah said that she didn't know how to bake bread.

T   F   b)   Anna was worried that Sarah might not come because she loved the sea so much.

T   F   c)   Caleb's letter from Sarah had a picture of a dolphin on the envelope.

T   F   d)   In her letter, Sarah had to admit she had difficulty keeping a fire going at night.

T   F   e)   About the only place Caleb didn't read his letter from Sarah was in his bed at night.

T   F   f)   Caleb suggested that they write back and tell Sarah they would like her to come.

2.   **Number the events from ❶ to ❻ in the order they occurred in these chapters.**

☐   **a)**   Anna receives a letter from Sarah.

☐   **b)**   They receive a letter from Sarah saying she would like to come to visit them.

☐   **c)**   Caleb, Anna and Papa write letters to Sarah.

☐   **d)**   Papa writes back to Sarah saying they would like her to come.

☐   **e)**   Caleb reads the book about sea birds over and over.

☐   **f)**   Caleb gets a letter from Sarah with Seal's footprints enclosed.

Chapter Two

Answer each question with a complete sentence.

1. In Sarah's letter to Anna, what three kinds of fish did Sarah say that her brother William caught?

_____

_____

2. Why did Caleb think he shouldn't have told Sarah that their house was small?

_____

_____

3. Where was the place on their farm that Papa chose to break the news about Sarah coming?

_____

_____

4. For how long was she planning to come?

_____

_____

5. What <u>three</u> things did Sarah write to describe how she would look when she arrived?

_____

_____

6. What had Sarah written at the bottom of her last letter?

_____

_____

Journaling Prompt

Imagine that you are Sarah. You have been invited to come out west to live with Anna and her family. What must Sarah have been feeling as she was making up her mind? Write a journal entry to describe her feelings at this difficult time in her life. Try to express two or three reasons for moving and two or three reasons why she shouldn't.

Chapter Three

1. What is meant to form a **_first impression_** of someone?

_____

_____

_____

2. In your opinion, what is most difficult thing about meeting new people? Please explain your answer.

_____

_____

_____

Vocabulary

Complete each sentence with a word from the list.

preacher	quilt	paintbrush	alarm	hitched
windmill	clattered	woodchuck	chores	suspend

1. The old woman was going to _____ the bucket over top of the well.

2. I'm sure that a _____ must have got into our vegetable garden.

3. Are you going to help your sister with the _____, Caleb?

4. A loud crack of thunder will _____ just about anyone.

5. The horse and buggy_____ into the yard, disturbing all of the chickens.

6. "Don't you think you should ask the _____ if he will marry you?" Anna asked.

7. They spread the _____ over my parents' bed.

8. The_____ is a source of power on the farm.

9. She _____ the horses to the buggy.

10. "Be sure to clean that _____ off good or it will be ruined," his dad told him.

Chapter Three

1. Answer each question with a word from the chapters.

a) Sarah came in the season of _____.

b) It took Papa a whole _____ to get to the train and back.

c) Papa's two horses were called _____ and _____.

d) The name of Sarah's cat was _____.

e) Sarah told them that the _____ fly high and drop the shells on the rocks below.

2. Use the words in the box to fill in the blanks.

paintbrush	mice	moon	olive	yellow

a) When Sara came Indian _____ covered the prairie.

b) Sarah was wearing a _____ bonnet.

c) Mama had planted the Russian _____ years ago.

d) Papa said that the cat would be good in the barn for _____.

e) The shell that Sarah gave Caleb was called a _____ snail.

After You Read 📖

Chapter Three

Answer each question with a complete sentence.

1. Why do you think Papa brushed his hair, and wore a clean blue shirt when he went to meet Sarah?

_____

_____

2. List any three of the chores Anna and Caleb did while they waited for their dad and Sarah to return.

_____

_____

3. Describe the gift that Sarah gave to Anna.

_____

_____

4. How was it formed?

_____

_____

5. How did the land around the farm remind Sarah of the sea?

_____

_____

6. What had the children seen in Sarah's look that made them think the preacher might not come to marry Sarah and Papa?

_____

_____

Journaling Prompt

Meeting Papa, Anna and Caleb must have been a very exciting event for Sarah. Describe her feelings in a journal entry at the end of this first day on the Witting farm.

NAME: _____

Chapter Four

1. What activity would you suggest doing with someone you wanted to get to know better? Explain your choice.

_____

_____

_____

Vocabulary

Word List

Anna
bonnet
bread
Caleb
clams
clover
conch
cup
curls
flower
hair
house
lamb
Maine
nests
Nick
Papa
pie
prairie
risk
roses
Sarah
sea
Seal
sheep
shell
shore
summer

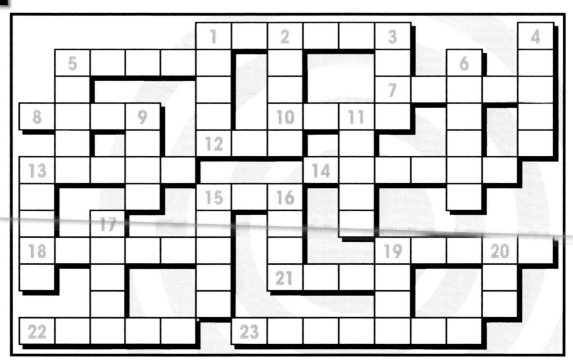

Across

1. One of the four seasons.
5. ___ Plain and Tall.
7. The edge of the ocean or a lake.
8. The name of Sarah's cat.
10. The name of one of the dogs in the novel.
12. A dessert often made from fruit.
13. Creatures of the sea with a shell.
14. An example of one is a *rose*.
15. ___ and saucer.
18. Lucky ones have 4 leaves – most have 3.
19. Caleb and Anna lived in one of these.
21. Caleb's sister.
22. Birds build these.
23. Where the Wittings lived.

Down

1. Wooly animals.
2. The state Sarah was from.
3. Hazard or danger.
4. Made from a cereal like wheat.
5. A sea ___.
6. A woman's head covering.
9. A baby sheep.
11. Anna's brother.
13. A spiraled shell.
15. Ringlets of hair.
16. Caleb called his father by this name.
17. These flowers are often red, pink or white.
19. Its homonym is *hare*.
20. Sarah lived near this for most of her life.

Chapter Four

1. Complete the paragraphs by filling in each blank with the correct word from the chapters.

The dogs loved _____ first. The dogs' names were
     a

_____ and _____. No one knew where
 b   **c**

_____ slept, for she was a _____. If you put a
 d   **e**

_____ shell to your _____ you could hear the
 f   **g**

_____. Papa and Anna were both quiet and _____
 h   **i**

with Sarah. Caleb, however, talked to her from _____ until
      j

the light left the sky. Sarah, Anna and Caleb picked flowers, paintbrushes

and clover and prairie _____. Anna knew that summer
     k

was when the _____ might be. They hung the flowers
   l

from the _____ in little bunches. Caleb made up a song
  m

about _____ ragwort. In Maine the word *ayuh* means
  n

_____. Sarah told them that her brother, William, had a boat
 o

called _____. After Sarah cut _____ hair she
  p   **q**

scattered the curls on the fence and on the _____. She said
         r

it was for the _____. After brushing Anna's hair she tied it with
   s

a rose _____ ribbon she brought from _____.
  t   **u**

Although Sarah admitted that she had never touched a _____,
           v

she said she had touched real _____.
      w

Chapter Four

Answer each question with a complete sentence.

1. Name three of the types of shells from Sarah's collection.

_____

_____

2. Why do you think she brought her shell collection with her?

_____

_____

3. How did Sarah plan to go about keeping flowers all winter long?

_____

_____

4. Why did Caleb think it was significant that Sarah said *winter*?

_____

_____

5. Why did Caleb smile at the name of the bride's bonnet flower?

_____

_____

6. What was unusual about Sarah's three aunts?

_____

_____

Journaling Prompt

It is plain that Caleb really wants Sarah to stay and looks for little hints in what she says and does to convince him of this. Write a journal entry from Caleb expressing the thoughts he must have been feeling at the end of Chapter Four.

NAME: _____

Chapter Five

1. Growing up on a farm can be a lot of fun. Think of two or three fun activities that farm children would probably enjoying doing.

_____

_____

2. The last chapter ended on a kind of sad note, didn't it? Sarah is missing home and wishing that she could touch a seal. Predict what you think will happen in Chapter 5. Will Sarah start to feel more comfortable on the Witting farm, or will she become even lonelier?

_____

_____

Vocabulary

Synonyms are words with similar meanings. Use the context of the sentences below to help you choose the best synonym for the underlined word in each sentence. If you cannot determine the meaning from the context, consult a dictionary.

1. Nick <u>crept</u> up behind the old horse and threw a saddle over its back.

    a) snuck   b) ran   c) jumped   d) galloped

2. The wool she used for the sweater was very <u>coarse</u>.

    a) expensive   b) rough   c) delicate   d) red

3. No one knew if there was a treasure buried in the <u>mound</u> of hay.

    a) porter   b) blanket   c) pile   d) barn

4. The fisherman's coat was made from <u>canvas</u>.

    a) nylon   b) rubber   c) leather   d) heavy cloth

5. "We have a lot of <u>dunes</u> in Maine," Sarah told them.

    a) boats   b) towns   c) piles   d) rocks

6. She fell asleep in the middle of the <u>meadow</u>.

    a) bed   b) field   c) lake   d) lane

7. "I don't know the answer," she <u>exclaimed</u>.

    a) blurted   b) whispered   c) lied   d) frowned

Chapter Five

1. **Put a check mark (✓) next to the answer that is most correct.**

a) Sarah named the three sheep:

○ **A** Harriet, Mattie and Lou
○ **B** Winken, Blinken and Nod
○ **C** Larry, Moe and Curly
○ **D** Sam, Joe and Wimpie

b) Sarah sang the following song to the sheep:

○ **A** *Dixie*
○ **B** *Red River Valley*
○ **C** *The Bonnie Blue Flag*
○ **D** *Sumer Is Icumen In*

c) What birds came to eat the lamb that had died?

○ **A** seagulls
○ **B** ravens
○ **C** turkey buzzards
○ **D** crows

d) What did Sarah use to draw her pictures with?

○ **A** charcoal
○ **B** crayons
○ **C** oil paints
○ **D** pencils

e) What was Caleb's first word?

○ **A** flower
○ **B** windmill
○ **C** Mama
○ **D** Papa

After You Read 📖

Chapter Five

Answer each question with a complete sentence.

1. Why do you think that Sarah's first word was *dune*?

_____

_____

2. <u>Investigate</u>: Sarah says that her dune sparkled with bits of mica. What is **mica**?

_____

_____

3. What kind of dune did Papa show them? How was it different than Sarah's?

_____

_____

4. Why did Papa keep his *dune* covered with canvas?

_____

_____

5. Describe the fun that Sarah and the children had on Papa's *dune*.

_____

_____

6. Why did Caleb think it was important that Sarah described the dune as ***our*** dune?

_____

_____

Journaling Prompt

Literary devices are important for a writer to use to make his/her writing more interesting for the reader. One kind of literary device is the simile – where the writer compares two things using the words *like* or *as*. An example of this is found in chapter five when the author writes, *the stars blinked like fireflies.* Here the author is comparing stars and fireflies. In your journal compose four more examples of similes. Try to use the characters and events of *Sarah, Plain and Tall* as your inspiration for creating these comparisons.

Chapter Six

1. What are some fun things to do in the snow?

_____

_____

_____

2. Of all the farm animals you can think of, which ones do you think would be the most fun to have around? Why?

_____

_____

_____

Vocabulary

Choose a word from the list to complete each definition.

gully	tumbleweed	killdeer	sharply	stiff
gleam	collapse	tread	sleeve	chant

1. To speak *sternly* is to speak _____.

2. To utter words or sounds in musical tones is to _____.

3. To have a breakdown is to _____.

4. A part of one's shirt or blouse is a _____.

5. A _____ is a small valley.

6. To _____ *lightly* means to walk without a sound.

7. To _____ is to shine.

8. A _____ blows across the prairie on a windy day.

9. A _____ is a type of bird.

10. The word _____ means *rigid* or *form*.

Chapter Six

1. **Circle T if the statement is TRUE or F if it is FALSE.**

T F **a)** The cows moved close to the pond because the water was cool there and there were trees.

T F **b)** Papa refused to teach Sarah how to plow the fields because he thought plowing was a man's work.

T F **c)** Jack the horse was always eager to work.

T F **d)** It was three miles to the local school.

T F **e)** During bad storms Papa tied a rope from the house to the barn so no one would get lost.

T F **f)** Unlike the water of the cow pond, the sea is salty.

2. **Number the events from ❶ to ❻ in the order they occurred in the chapters.**

☐ **a)** Sarah takes off her dress and wades into the cow pond in her petticoat.

☐ **b)** The sun rises higher, and Papa stops to take off his hat and wipe his face with his sleeve.

☐ **c)** Caleb and Anna tell Sarah about winter.

☐ **d)** Sarah tries to teach Anna and Caleb how to swim.

☐ **e)** Caleb runs like the wind with the sheep following him.

☐ **f)** Sarah suggests that they go in for a swim.

NAME: _____

Chapter Six

Answer each question with a complete sentence.

1. From Anna and Caleb's description of winter, what do you think would be one thing you would enjoy about such a winter?

_____

_____

2. What do you think would be one thing you would <u>not</u> likely enjoy?

_____

_____

3. Sarah said that she was good at *sums* and *writing*. What did she mean by *sums*?

_____

_____

4. Why did Caleb jokingly suggest to Sarah that in Maine they could have a cow to Sunday supper?

_____

_____

5. Find an example of exaggeration from Anna's description of winter on the prairies.

_____

_____

6. <u>Put your detective hat on</u>. It mentions in Chapter 5 that Sarah named the sheep after her three aunts. It then goes on to say that one of the lambs died. We don't know for sure, but what <u>may</u> have been the name of the sheep that died? What clues did you discover?

_____

_____

Journaling Prompt

Imagine you are either Sarah, Anna or Caleb and write a journal entry describing the events of Chapter 6.

Chapter Seven

1. "Loneliness adds beauty to life. It puts a special burn on sunsets and makes night air smell better." (Henry Rollins) Do you think Sarah would agree with this quote by Henry Rollins? Support your answer.

_____

_____

2. Flowers and gardens are an important part of this chapter. Why do you think people keep flower gardens? What flowers do you think you would grow in your own personal garden?

_____

_____

Vocabulary

Circle the correct word that matches the meaning of the underlined word.

1. My aunt sat very <u>primly</u> at the dinner table.

    a) impatiently   b) properly   c) sympathetically   d) playfully

2. Susan <u>shuffled</u> tiredly into the classroom.

    a) shambled   b) tripped   c) skipped   d) stumbled

3. Papa will <u>hitch</u> it up properly before he leaves.

    a) fence   b) lift   c) gate   d) connect

4. There was a lone <u>marigold</u> on the kitchen floor.

    a) a sunbeam   b) a piglet   c) a flower   d) a tomato plant

5. Their bellies were full of <u>greens</u> and biscuits.

    a) vegetables   b) grass   c) oats   d) corn

6. "I will give you more. I have <u>tansy</u>," Maggie said.

    a) the flu   b) a pet banty chicken c) a small flower pot d) a weedy herb

NAME: _____

Chapter Seven

1. Fill in each blank with the correct word from the chapter.

a) The Wittings' neighbors, _____ and Maggie came to help Papa plow.

b) Papa had picked wild _____ for Sarah.

c) _____ loved the chickens.

d) The children were named _____ and _____.

e) Maggie was originally from _____.

f) Maggie said that she would teach Sarah how to drive a _____.

2. Use the words in the box to fill in the blanks.

garden	three	Mama	dahlias	quilt	two

a) Matthew and his wife brought their _____ children and _____ chickens.

b) They covered the big table with a _____.

c) Anna said that she missed _____.

d) Maggie told Sarah that she must have a _____.

e) In Sarah's garden in Maine she grew _____ and columbine.

NAME: _____

Chapter Seven

Answer each question with a complete sentence.

1. Why did the Wittings' neighbors bring three extra horses to help plow the field, instead of just the two pulling their wagon?

_____

_____

2. How do you think Maggie knew that Sarah was lonely?

_____

_____

3. How did Maggie try to comfort Sarah and encourage her?

_____

_____

4. Investigate: Maggie brought Sarah three types of plants for her garden – **zinnias, marigolds** and **wild feverfew**. Using the school library or Internet research <u>one</u> of these flowers and write a brief description of it below.

_____

_____

_____

5. Why did Anna know that the chickens would not be for eating?

_____

_____

_____

6. Why wasn't it possible for Sarah to walk to town from where she <u>now</u> lived?

_____

_____

Journaling Prompt

Imagine that after returning home Maggie made an entry into her journal expressing her thoughts on her new friend, Sarah. What might she write about her first impressions of this young lady from Maine?

Chapter Eight

1. In Chapter 8 we get to see another side of Sarah. We see that she is very brave and that she has *a mind of her own*. What do we mean by the expression, **having a mind of your own**? Describe how this can be a good thing.

_____

_____

_____

2. How do you think a bad storm can be a terrible thing for a farmer?

_____

_____

Vocabulary

Write a complete sentence using the following words. Make sure that the meaning of each word is clear in your sentence.

argument _____

crisply _____

overalls _____

wisps _____

portion _____

pungent _____

squall _____

weary _____

eerie _____

NAME: _____

Chapter Eight

1. Complete the paragraphs by filling in each blank with the correct word from the chapters.

Sarah, dressed in overalls, went to the barn to have an _____ with Papa.
  a
She also took _____ for Old Bess and _____. Caleb
  b   **c**
thought that women shouldn't wear _____. Sarah also wanted to learn
  d
how to ride a _____ and drive a _____.
  e   **f**
Sarah wanted to ride Jack, but _____ said "Not Jack." Papa told
  g
Sarah that they could start to practice _____. Sarah told Papa
  h
that she would help him to fix the _____, because she was a
  i
good _____. Anna and Caleb could hear the steady sound of
  j
_____ on the roof. When they were called outside, the children saw a
  k
huge, black _____ moving toward them.
  l
Papa ordered Caleb to bring the _____ inside the barn. He also
  m
ordered Anna to bring the _____ and the _____
  n   **o**
inside. The _____ was the safest building on the farm.
  p
_____ stood close by Anna, trembling.
  q

2. Choose the most appropriate answer for each of the following:

a) The children's faces looked _____ in the strange light:

_____ **A** yellow
_____ **B** dull
_____ **C** frightened
_____ **D** twisted

b) The only animals that didn't appear frightened by the storm were:

_____ **A** the dogs
_____ **B** the sheep
_____ **C** Seal and Jack
_____ **D** the chickens

c) Sarah ran into the storm to get:

_____ **A** Seal
_____ **B** the laundry
_____ **C** her chickens
_____ **D** Nick

d) At dawn it began to:

_____ **A** snow
_____ **B** hail
_____ **C** sleet
_____ **D** clear up

NAME: _____

Chapter Eight

Answer each question with a complete sentence.

1. Why do you think Sarah wanted to ride Jack in particular?

_____

_____

2. What do you think Papa meant when he said that Jack was *sly*?

_____

_____

3. Why do you think that Sarah wanted to go to town by herself?

_____

_____

4. <u>Investigate</u>: Look up the meaning of a **squall**. Why do you think it was it so frightening to the Wittings?

_____

_____

_____

5. What did Anna remember when she saw Papa and Sarah standing together during the squall?

_____

_____

_____

6. Do you think the storm helped Sarah to feel more a part of the Witting family? Explain your answer.

_____

Journaling Prompt

Have you ever lived through a big storm like Anna and Caleb did in this chapter? If so write about what it was like. If you haven't, try to imagine what it must be like to have such an adventure and describe it in a journal entry.

Chapter Nine

1. Chapter Nine is a very important part of the story of Anna and her family. It describes a most difficult experience for all members of the Witting household – even Sarah. Describe a time in your own life when you were kept on "pins and needles" waiting for something to happen. Describe your feelings and how it came about.

_____

_____

_____

2. How difficult do you think it was for Sarah to this point in the story to adapt to life in the Witting household? What might have made it easier than it was? What might have made it harder?

_____

_____

_____

Vocabulary

In each of the following sets of words, underline the one word which does not belong. Then write a sentence explaining why it does not fit.

1. a) complained b) grouched c) whined d) provoked

_____

2. a) stern b) harsh c) exhausted d) strict

_____

3. a) announced b) cried c) howled d) wailed

_____

4. a) dusk b) evening c) nightfall d) dirty

_____

5. a) damaged b) angry c) injured d) harmed

_____

Chapter Nine

1. Put a check mark (✓) next to the answer that is most correct.

a) What was the only thing badly damaged by the storm?

○ **A**   the fence around the cow pond

○ **B**   the barn roof

○ **C**   one field

○ **D**   the chicken coop

b) Caleb suggested this strategy for making Sarah stay:

○ **A**   tie her up

○ **B**   he could pretend to be sick

○ **C**   both A & B

○ **D**   none of the above

c) What did Sarah take on the wagon for Old Bess and Jack?

○ **A**   a barrel of water

○ **B**   some freshly cut flowers

○ **C**   a sack of oats

○ **D**   a bundle of hay

d) Who was left with the responsibility of looking after Seal?

○ **A**   Anna

○ **B**   Caleb

○ **C**   Papa

○ **D**   Both A & B

e) Who did Caleb say had been very worried about Sarah when she was gone?

○ **A**   Anna

○ **B**   Papa

○ **C**   Seal

○ **D**   her three chickens

After You Read 📖

Chapter Nine

Answer each question with a complete sentence.

1. Why were both Anna and Caleb so upset about Sarah going into town alone?

_____

_____

2. What did Sarah do when she left for town that surprised Papa?

_____

_____

3. Who did Anna think of as Sarah left – and why?

_____

_____

4. Why did Anna think that Sarah might indeed be coming back?

_____

_____

_____

5. What was the first sign that Sarah was returning to the farm?

_____

_____

_____

6. What gift did Sarah return with? Why did Caleb say that Sarah had returned with the sea?

_____

_____

_____

Journaling Prompt

This was a most stressful day for the Witting family. Imagine that you are Papa, Anna or Caleb and write a journal entry describing the emotions you felt when Sarah was in town, and how it made you feel when she returned.

Review - Chapters One to Nine

Vocabulary Review

Choose a word from the list that means the same as the underlined word(s).

horrible	stubborn	huddle	mica	stroke	insult
rustle	sly	energetic	weary	pesky	petticoat

1. I certainly didn't mean to <u>offend</u> your sister by saying she looked tired. _____

2. Caleb was one of the most <u>active</u> boys you will ever meet. _____

3. Jake was a very <u>sneaky</u> horse. _____

4. The dress made a <u>soft sound</u> as she entered the room. _____

5. She sprinkled the small pieces of <u>mineral</u> on to the picture. _____

6. All she was wearing was her <u>underskirt</u> when she jumped into the cow pond.

    _____

7. She was a most <u>obstinate</u> child. _____

8. It was a <u>terrible</u> accident. _____

9. She asked everyone in her class to <u>squat</u> down on the floor around her and listen intently.

    _____

10. The doctor was very <u>tired</u> after working in the Emergency Ward all night. _____

11. The little dog was the most <u>bothersome</u> pet I have ever seen. _____

12. She began to gently <u>pat</u> the old horse on the nose. _____

Review - Chapters One to Nine

Design a new and attractive cover for the novel, *Sarah, Plain and Tall*. It should feature the title, the author's name, and an appropriate picture from the novel (perhaps your favorite scene). Make sure to color the picture.

Review - Chapters One to Nine

Answer each question with a complete sentence.

1. What is meant by the **climax** of a novel? When does it usually occur in the book?

_____

_____

2. When do you think the climax of **Sarah, Plain and Tall** occurs? Why do you believe this?

_____

_____

3. Who was your favorite character in the novel? Why?

_____

_____

4. Describe your favorite scene.

_____

_____

_____

5. Do you think Sarah will make a good wife for Papa, and a good mother for Anna and Caleb? Defend your answer.

_____

_____

_____

6. What difficulties might the Witting family still have, even now that Sarah has made up her mind to stay with them?

_____

_____

_____

Journaling Prompt

As a final journal entry, write your final impressions of the book. How would it rate among your favorites?

Chapter 1

Tercets

Tercets are poems with <u>three lines</u>. For this exercise you may choose which lines will rhyme.

Here is an example of a tercet poem.

> **DANCING SHOES**
> With pink dancing shoes,
> She can't sing the blues,
> No matter how sad she may feel.

Now try your hand at writing a **tercet** using the events of Chapter 1 for inspiration. Some suggestions for topics: parents, favorite songs, living on a farm, younger brothers (or older sisters), babies. You may, of course, write more than one 3-line stanza for your tercet poem.

- -

Chapters 2 - 3

A Letter Home

Sarah is a real letter-writer. Soon after arriving at the Wittings she no doubt sat down and wrote home to her brother and his new wife, as well as to her old aunts. What would she say in such letters? Would she describe the Wittings? Her new home on the prairies? The wildflowers and unusual animals she had seen? Certainly she would give her impressions of her new life and how she was adapting. Imagine you are Sarah and pen such a letter back home to your family. Be sure to describe some of your impressions and feelings about this momentous adventure that you have undertaken – and perhaps even what you feel your plans for the future might be.

Chapters 4 - 5

A Comic Strip

This activity is especially for students with an artistic flair or who love comic books! It can be done for events included in Chapters 4 - 5 or for Chapters 1 - 5. The first step is to decide on the length of your comic strip (6 to 12 frames is suggested); next consider what events you will include. You may wish to highlight a brief incident (i.e. Sarah's arrival at the farm), or encompass the highlights of the novel to this point. You may even want to provide an alternate ending to the scene!

A quick sketch of the comic strip can first be accomplished in a **storyboard format** before a final, good copy is attempted. The strip should include a title, dialog, and color. It should be neat and imaginative.

📋 Writing Task # 4

Chapters 6 - 7

An anagram is a word that is formed by changing the order of the letters of another word. For example, the letters of the word EACH can also form the word ACHE.

Follow the directions to form the anagrams: a) Read the clue in the right-hand column. b) Using the word in the left-hand column – move the letters around in any order – but you must use all the letters.

Word	Anagram	Clue
THREE		A number.
OVER		To wander.
GARDEN		Peril.
EAT		A drink.
HORSE		Edge of the sea.
MARRIED		Someone who likes you.

Chapters 8 - 9

The Interview

You are the editor of a newspaper in the town near the Witting farm. You have heard the fascinating story of Sarah's arrival and are anxious to discover how she and the family are doing. You believe that this will make for interesting reading in your weekly paper. You arrange to meet with Sarah to do an interview for the next edition of **The Prairie Talespinner.**

Prepare at least <u>five</u> interesting questions to ask Sarah about her experiences. You should also include Sarah's answers to these questions. These answers should reveal something of Sarah's extraordinary character, perhaps give details of her past that helped prepare her for her journey west to live with the Wittings – and perhaps marry Jacob Witting.

(You may, if you wish, choose to interview another member of the Witting family: Papa, Anna or Caleb.)

Chapters 1 - 9

Critical Review!

Your assignment is to write a brief review of **Sarah, Plain and Tall** for posting on a website such as www.amazon.com. This review can be about the novel itself, or the movie version that you have seen. This is an opportunity to share your opinion of the novel with other young people who are deciding whether or not to read it.

Your review should be at least two paragraphs in length. One paragraph should briefly describe the plot (without giving away the ending). The second paragraph should give your impression of the novel.

When writing your impression, try to include one favorable comment and one suggestion as to how the novel might be improved.

Word Search Puzzle

Find the 16 words from the Word Box in the Word Search Puzzle. The words are in a straight line, but can be forwards, backwards, or even diagonal.

BISCUIT	FIREFLY	MARIGOLD	PREFER
CHICKEN	HAILSTONE	MEADOW	SARAH
CHORES	INSECTS	PITCHFORK	SCALLOP
DUNES	INSULT	PRAIRIE	WOODCHUCK

W	W	E	R	T	Y	K	R	O	F	H	C	T	I	P
O	I	A	S	B	I	S	C	U	I	T	A	S	D	F
O	N	N	Z	X	C	E	N	O	T	S	L	I	A	H
D	E	Q	S	C	M	E	A	D	O	W	V	B	N	P
C	K	Q	W	U	L	R	T	Y	U	I	O	P	R	A
H	C	A	S	D	L	F	G	H	J	K	L	E	Z	X
U	I	C	V	S	B	T	N	M	Q	W	F	E	R	T
C	H	A	E	S	D	F	S	G	H	E	J	K	F	T
K	C	N	Z	X	C	A	V	B	R	N	M	E	I	P
X	U	C	M	A	R	I	G	O	L	D	I	Z	R	O
D	X	C	C	A	V	B	N	M	N	R	M	Q	E	L
A	S	D	H	F	G	H	J	K	I	L	T	Y	F	L
I	N	S	E	C	T	S	W	A	E	R	T	Y	L	A
S	D	F	G	C	H	O	R	E	S	G	H	J	Y	C
Z	X	C	V	B	N	P	N	M	Q	W	E	R	T	S

Comprehension Quiz

28

Answer each question in a complete sentence.

1. How had Anna and Caleb's mother died?

_____

_____

2

2. Describe the circumstances which led to Sarah traveling west to join the Wittings.

_____

_____

2

3. What kind of animal did Sarah bring with her, and what was its name?

_____

_____

2

4. What had been Anna's impression of her younger brother when Caleb had been born?

_____

_____

2

5. Where was Sarah from and who did she live with before moving west?

_____

_____

2

6. What did the children notice that their father stopped doing after their mother died?

_____

_____

2

7. What **dune** did they find on the farm, and what activity did Sarah lead Anna and Caleb in there?

_____

_____

2

SUBTOTAL: **/14**

Comprehension Quiz

8. Matthew and Maggie brought Sarah a gift (in a sack). What was in the sack?

_____

_____

    2

9. How did Maggie attempt to help Sarah?

_____

_____

    2

10. What was Sarah able to get Papa to do once again – something he hadn't done since his wife died?

_____

_____

    2

11. Why did Papa refuse to teach Sarah how to ride Jack?

_____

_____

    2

12. How was Sarah a big help just before the squall hit the farm?

_____

_____

    2

13. Why were the children so upset when Sarah decided to go into town by herself?

_____

_____

    2

14. What gift did Sarah bring for Anna and Caleb when she returned from town?

_____

_____

    2

SUBTOTAL: /14

1.
a) **F**
b) **T**
c) **F**
d) **F**
e) **F**
f) **T**

2.
a) 2
b) 5
c) 1
d) 6
e) 3
f) 4

(15)

1. Flounder, sea bass, bluefish.

2. Sarah might decide not to come.

3. The barn/horse stalls.

4. A month.

5. She will wear a yellow bonnet. She is plain and tall.

6. Tell them I sing.

(16)

---

1. Answers will vary

2. Answers will vary

Vocabulary

1. a type of fish
2. annoying
3. choose
4. a hair style
5. farm instrument
6. a compartment in a stable
7. moist
8. surround
9. overwhelm with surprise
10. smile
11. a woman's hat
12. roof covering

(14)

1. Answers will vary

2. Answers will vary. He was sad and worn with responsibilities.

3. Their mother had died the morning after Caleb was born.

4. To get a mail order bride.

5. Probably in case she wasn't interested. He didn't want to get their hopes up.

6. Ask her if she sings. Answers will vary.

(13)

1.
a) ◯ B
b) ◯ C
c) ◯ B
d) ◯ D
e) ◯ A

(12)

1. Answers will vary

2. Answers will vary

Vocabulary

1. dusk
2. homely
3. feisty
4. harsh
5. insult
6. troublesome
7. familiar
8. wretched
9. colt
10. advertisement

(11)

Page 17

1. Answers will vary
2. Answers will vary

Vocabulary
1. suspend
2. woodchuck
3. chores
4. alarm
5. clattered
6. preacher
7. quilt
8. windmill
9. hitched
10. paintbrush

(17)

Page 18

1.
a) spring
b) day
c) Old Bess and Jack
d) Seal
e) Mother

2.
a) paintbrush
b) yellow
c) olive
d) mice
e) moon

(18)

Page 19

1. Answers may vary. (i.e. he wanted to make a good impression.)
2. Any 3 of: shoveled the stalls; laid down new hay; fed sheep; swept; carried wood and water.
3. A sea stone
4. The sea washed over it until it is perfectly round.
5. The land rolled a little like the sea.
6. Loneliness.

(19)

Page 20

1. Answers will vary

Vocabulary

Across
1. summer
5. Sarah
7. shore
8. seal
10. Nick
12. pie
13. clams
14. flower
15. cup
18. clover
19. house
21. Anna
22. nests
23. prairie

Down
1. sheep
2. Maine
3. risk
4. bread
5. shell
6. bonnet
9. lamb
11. Caleb
13. conch
15. curls
16. Papa
17. roses
19. hair
20. sea

(20)

Page 21

1.
a. Sarah
b. Lottie   c. Nick
d. Seal   e. roamer
f. conch g. ear
h. sea   i. shy
j. morning
k. violets
l. wedding
m. ceiling
n. wooly
o. yes
p. Kittiwake
q. Caleb's
r. ground
s. birds
t. velvet u. Maine
v. sheep
w. seals

(21)

Page 22

1. Three of: scallop, sea clam, oyster, razor clam, conch shell.
2. Answers will vary. (i.e. to remind her of home)
3. Hang them upside down and dry them.
4. It meant she would stay.
5. Sarah would soon be a bride.
6. They wear silk dresses and no shoes.

(22)

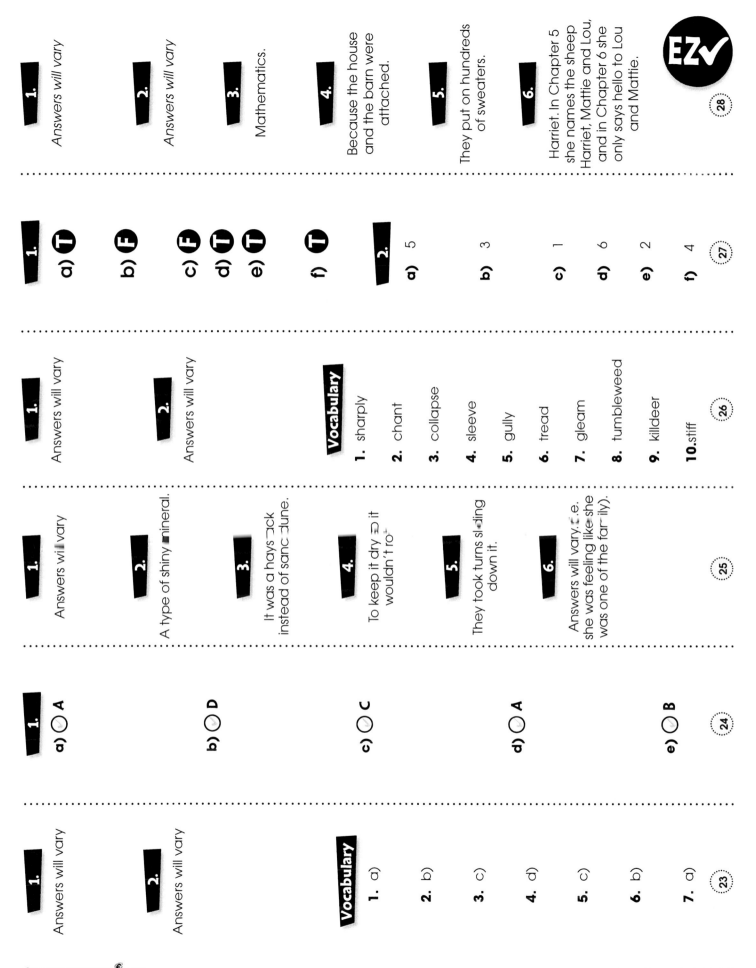

1. Answers will vary
2. Answers will vary
3. Mathematics.
4. Because the house and the barn were attached.
5. They put on hundreds of sweaters.
6. Harriet. In Chapter 5 she names the sheep Harriet, Mattie and Lou, and in Chapter 6 she only says hello to Lou and Mattie.

EZ✓ 28

1.
a) T
b) F
c) F
d) T
e) T
f) T

2.
a) 5
b) 3
c) 1
d) 6
e) 2
f) 4

27

1. Answers will vary
2. Answers will vary

Vocabulary
1. sharply
2. chant
3. collapse
4. sleeve
5. gully
6. tread
7. gleam
8. tumbleweed
9. killdeer
10. stiff

26

1. Answers will vary
2. A type of shiny mineral.
3. It was a haystack instead of sand dune.
4. To keep it dry so it wouldn't rot.
5. They took turns sliding down it.
6. Answers will vary. i.e. she was feeling like she was one of the family).

25

1.
a) ◯ A
b) ◯ D
c) ◯ C
d) ◯ A
e) ◯ B

24

1. Answers will vary
2. Answers will vary

Vocabulary
1. a)
2. b)
3. c)
4. d)
5. c)
6. b)
7. a)

23

29

1. Answers will vary

2. Answers will vary

Vocabulary
1. b)
2. d)
3. d)
4. c)
5. a)
6. d)

30

1.
a) Matthew
b) daisies
c) Sarah
d) Rose, Violet
e) Tennessee
f) wagon

2.
a) two, three
b) quilt
c) Mama
d) garden
e) dahlias

31

1. Papa needed 5 horses for the big gang plow.

2. She had left Tennessee to come to the Prairie and missed her hometown too.

3. She told her there are always things to miss no matter where you are.

4. Answers will vary

5. Sarah named the chickens.

6. Town was too far away to walk.

32

1. Answers will vary

2. Answers will vary

Vocabulary
Answers will vary

33

1.
a) argument
b) apples
c) Jack
d) overalls
e) horse
f) wagon
g) Papa
h) tomorrow
i) roof
j) carpenter
k) pounding
l) cloud
m) horses
n) sheep
o) cows
p) barn
q) Mattie

2.
a) ○ A
b) ⬤ D
c) ⬤ C
d) ○ B

34

1. Jack was her favorite.

2. Answers will vary

3. Answers will vary

4. Answers will vary

5. She remembered her Papa and Mama standing like that.

6. Answers will vary

EZ✓

40

1. The climax is the highest point in a novel and usually occurs near the end and when the story's most important problem is solved.

2. When Sarah returns from town and the children realize she is there to stay.

3. Answers will vary

4. Answers will vary

5. Answers will vary

6. Answers will vary. (They are a pioneer family living with many hardships – crops might fail, family members get sick, animals might die)

39

Answers will vary

Vocabulary

1. insult
2. energetic
3. sly
4. rustle
5. mica
6. petticoat
7. stubborn
8. horrible
9. huddle
10. weary
11. pesky
12. stroke

38

1. They thought she wasn't going to come back.

2. She kissed him.

3. She thought of her Mama. She remembered the day a wagon took her Mama away and she never came back.

4. Because her coat Seal was still there.

5. The first sign was the dog, "Nick" jumping off the porch and running down the road.

6. She bought colored pencils for them to color the sea in her drawing.

37

a) ◯ C

b) ◯ C

c) ◯ D

d) ◯ D

e) ◯ C

36

1. Answers will vary

2. Answers will vary

Vocabulary

1. d)
2. c)
3. a)
4. d)
5. b) Explanations will vary

35

Word Search Puzzle

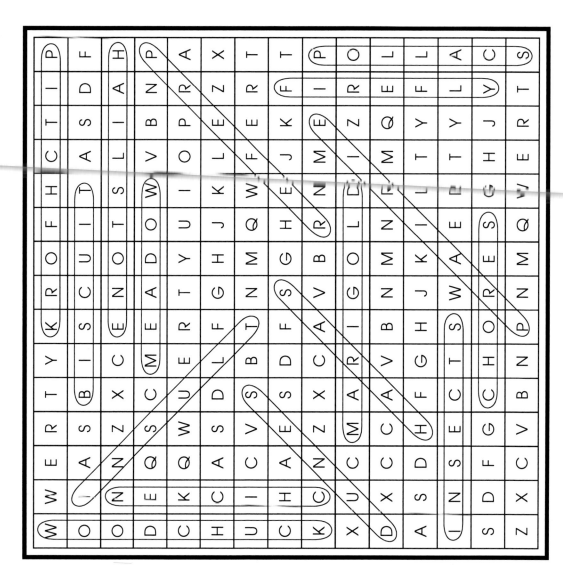

8.
Three chickens.

9.
She encouraged her, brought her chickens and flowers and offered to teach her to drive a wagon.

10.
Sing.

11.
Jack was sly (mean).

12.
She helped Papa fix the house roof in a hurry.

13.
They thought she might not return.

14.
Three colored pencils.

1.
She died of complications after giving birth to Caleb.

2.
Papa put an ad in a newspaper asking for a wife to come and join their family. Sarah responded to the ad and came west.

3.
A cat named Seal.

4.
She thought he was homely, plain, hollered and smelled.

5.
She was from Maine and she lived with her brother, William.

6.
Singing.

7.
A haystack. Sliding down it.

Comparison Chart

Sarah's former home was quite different from her new home with the Wittings, wasn't it? In the chart below consider each item listed under CRITERIA and fill in the details for Sarah's old and new homes.

CRITERIA	FORMER HOME	NEW HOME
With whom did Sarah live?		
Where was the home located?		
What did the people in her household do for a living?		
What is the climate like?		
What is the land like around here (geography)?		
What is the vegetation like here?		

Making up Sarah's Mind

It must have been very difficult for Sarah to decide whether or not to stay with the Wittings. She came as a complete stranger and within one short month was expected to decide her future for the rest of her life. Surely during this time a lot of thoughts and arguments went through her mind – both for staying and for going back to Maine. Imagine you are Sarah. Using the chart below, list as many reasons both for staying and for leaving as you can think of. Then place a star beside one or two of the best reasons in each category.

WHY I SHOULD STAY	WHY I SHOULD LEAVE

Sequence Chart

List the **main** events of *Sarah, Plain and Tall* in the order in which they occurred.

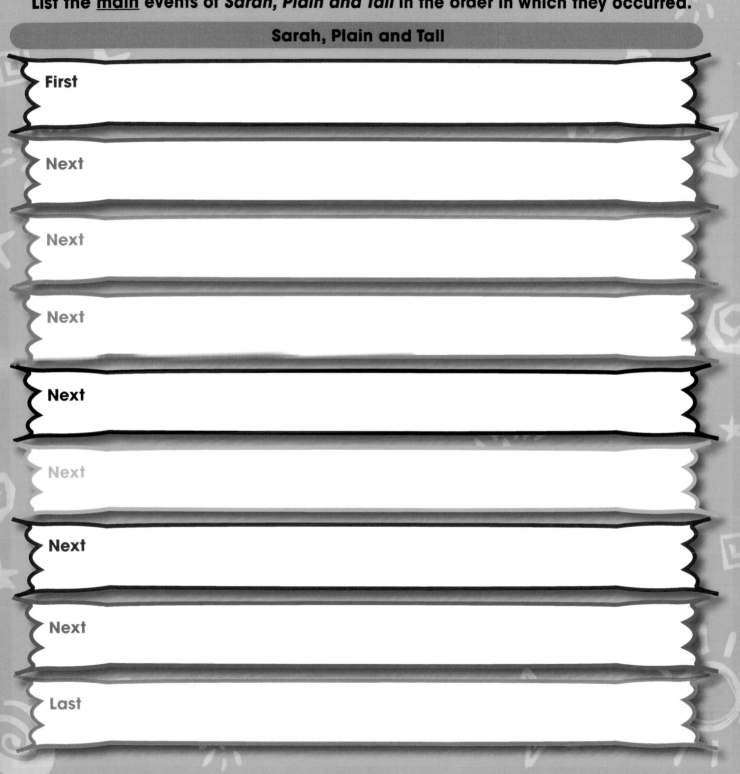

Sarah, Plain and Tall

First

Next

Next

Next

Next

Next

Next

Next

Last

Sarah, Plain and Tall CC2308

- **RSL.3.1** Ask and answer questions to demonstrate understanding of a text, referring explicitly to the text as the basis for the answers.
- **RSL.3.2** Recount stories, including fables, folktales, and myths from diverse cultures; determine the central message, lesson, or moral and explain how it is conveyed through key details in the text.
- **RSL.3.3** Describe characters in a story and explain how their actions contribute to the sequence of events.
- **RSL.3.4** Determine the meaning of words and phrases as they are used in a text, distinguishing literal from non-literal language.
- **RSL.3.5** Refer to parts of stories, dramas, and poems when writing or speaking about a text, using terms such as chapter, scene, and stanza; describe how each successive part builds on earlier sections.
- **RSL.3.6** Distinguish their own point of view from that of the narrator or those of the characters.
- **RSL.3.7** Explain how specific aspects of a text's illustrations contribute to what is conveyed by the words in a story.
- **RSL.3.10** By the end of the year read and comprehend literature, including stories, dramas, and poetry, at the high end of the grades 2–3 text complexity band independently and proficiently.
- **RSL.4.1** Refer to details and examples in a text when explaining what the text says explicitly and when drawing inferences from the text.
- **RSL.4.2** Determine a theme of a story, drama, or poem from details in the text; summarize the text.
- **RSL.4.3** Describe in depth a character, setting, or event in a story or drama, drawing on specific details in the text.
- **RSL.4.4** Determine the meaning of words and phrases as they are used in a text, including those that allude to significant characters found in mythology.
- **RSL.4.6** Compare and contrast the point of view from which different stories are narrated, including the difference between first- and third-person narrations.
- **RSL.4.10** By the end of the year read and comprehend literature, including stories, dramas, and poetry, in the grades 4–5 text complexity band proficiently, with scaffolding as needed at the high end of the range.
- **RSFS.3.3** Know and apply grade-level phonics and word analysis skills in decoding words. **A)** Identify and know the meaning of the most common prefixes and derivational suffixes. **B)** Decode words with common Latin suffixes. **C)** Decode multi-syllable words. d. Read grade-appropriate irregularly spelled words.
- **RSFS.3.4** Read with sufficient accuracy and fluency to support comprehension. **A)** Read grade-level text with purpose and understanding. **B)**. Read grade-level prose and poetry orally with accuracy, appropriate rate, and expression on successive readings **C)** Use context to confirm or self-correct word recognition and understanding, rereading as necessary.
- **RSFS.4.3** Know and apply grade-level phonics and word analysis skills in decoding words. **A)** Use combined knowledge of all letter-sound correspondences, syllabication patterns, and morphology to read accurately unfamiliar multisyllabic words in context and out of context.
- **RSFS.4.4** Read with sufficient accuracy and fluency to support comprehension. **A)** Read grade-level text with purpose and understanding. **B)** Read grade-level prose and poetry orally with accuracy, appropriate rate, and expression on successive readings. **C)** Use context to confirm or self-correct word recognition and understanding, rereading as necessary.
- **WS.3.1** Write opinion pieces on topics or texts, supporting a point of view with reasons. **A)** Introduce the topic or text they are writing about, state an opinion, and create an organizational structure that lists reasons. **B)** Provide reasons that support the opinion. **C)** Use linking words and phrases to connect opinion and reasons. **D)** Provide a concluding statement or section.
- **WS.3.2** Write informative/explanatory texts to examine a topic and convey ideas and information clearly. **A)** Introduce a topic and group related information together; include illustrations when useful to aiding comprehension. **B)** Develop the topic with facts, definitions, and details. **C)** Use linking words and phrases to connect ideas within categories of information. **D)** Provide a concluding statement or section.
- **WS.3.3** Write narratives to develop real or imagined experiences or events using effective technique, descriptive details, and clear event sequences. **A)** Establish a situation and introduce a narrator and/or characters; organize an event sequence that unfolds naturally. **B)** Use dialogue and descriptions of actions, thoughts, and feelings to develop experiences and events or show the response of characters to situations. **C)** Use temporal words and phrases to signal event order. **D)** Provide a sense of closure.
- **WS.3.4** With guidance and support from adults, produce writing in which the development and organization are appropriate to task and purpose.
- **WS.3.7** Conduct short research projects that build knowledge about a topic.
- **WS.3.8** Recall information from experiences or gather information from print and digital sources; take brief notes on sources and sort evidence into provided categories.
- **WS.4.1** Write opinion pieces on topics or texts, supporting a point of view with reasons and information. **A)** Introduce a topic or text clearly, state an opinion, and create an organizational structure in which related ideas are grouped to support the writer's purpose. **B)** Provide reasons that are supported by facts and details. **C)** Link opinion and reasons using words and phrases. **D)** Provide a concluding statement or section related to the opinion presented.
- **WS.4.3** Write narratives to develop real or imagined experiences or events using effective technique, descriptive details, and clear event sequences. **A)** Orient the reader by establishing a situation and introducing a narrator and/or characters; organize an event sequence that unfolds naturally. **B)** Use dialogue and description to develop experiences and events or show the responses of characters to situations. **C)** Use a variety of transitional words and phrases to manage the sequence of events. **D)** Use concrete words and phrases and sensory details to convey experiences and events precisely. **E)** Provide a conclusion that follows from the narrated experiences or events.
- **WS.4.4** Produce clear and coherent writing in which the development and organization are appropriate to task, purpose, and audience.
- **WS.4.7** Conduct short research projects that build knowledge through investigation of different aspects of a topic.
- **WS.4.8** Recall relevant information from experiences or gather relevant information from print and digital sources; take notes and categorize information, and provide a list of sources.
- **WS.4.9** Draw evidence from literary or informational texts to support analysis, reflection, and research. **A)** Apply *grade 4 Reading standards* to literature. **B)** Apply *grade 4 Reading standards* to informational texts.

Publication Listing

Ask Your Dealer About Our Complete Line

VISIT:

www.CLASSROOM COMPLETE PRESS.com

To view sample pages from each book

SOCIAL STUDIES - Software

ITEM #	TITLE
	MAPPING SKILLS SERIES
CC7770	Grades PK-2 Mapping Skills with Google Earth
CC7771	Grades 3-5 Mapping Skills with Google Earth
CC7772	Grades 6-8 Mapping Skills with Google Earth
CC7773	Grades PK-8 Mapping Skills with Google Earth Big Box

SOCIAL STUDIES - Books

ITEM #	TITLE
	MAPPING SKILLS SERIES
CC5786	Grades PK-2 Mapping Skills with Google Earth
CC5787	Grades 3-5 Mapping Skills with Google Earth
CC5788	Grades 6-8 Mapping Skills with Google Earth
CC5789	Grades PK-8 Mapping Skills with Google Earth Big Book
	NORTH AMERICAN GOVERNMENTS SERIES
CC5757	American Government
CC5758	Canadian Government
CC5759	Mexican Government
CC5760	Governments of North America Big Book
	WORLD GOVERNMENTS SERIES
CC5761	World Political Leaders
CC5762	World Electoral Processes
CC5763	Capitalism vs. Communism
CC5777	World Politics Big Book
	WORLD CONFLICT SERIES
CC5511	American Revolutionary War
CC5500	American Civil War
CC5512	American Wars Big Book
CC5501	World War I
CC5502	World War II
CC5503	World Wars I & II Big Book
CC5505	Korean War
CC5506	Vietnam War
CC5507	Korean & Vietnam Wars Big Book
CC5508	Persian Gulf War (1990-1991)
CC5509	Iraq War (2003-2010)
CC5510	Gulf Wars Big Book
	WORLD CONTINENTS SERIES
CC5750	North America
CC5751	South America
CC5768	The Americas Big Book
CC5752	Europe
CC5753	Africa
CC5754	Asia
CC5755	Australia
CC5756	Antarctica
	WORLD CONNECTIONS SERIES
CC5782	Culture, Society & Globalization
CC5783	Economy & Globalization
CC5784	Technology & Globalization
CC5785	Globalization Big Book

REGULAR & REMEDIAL EDUCATION

Reading Level 3-4 Grades 5-8

ENVIRONMENTAL STUDIES - Software

ITEM #	TITLE
	CLIMATE CHANGE SERIES
CC7747	Global Warming: Causes Grades 3-8
CC7748	Global Warming: Effects Grades 3-8
CC7749	Global Warming: Reduction Grades 3-8
CC7750	Global Warming Big Box Grades 3-8

ENVIRONMENTAL STUDIES - Books

ITEM #	TITLE
	MANAGING OUR WASTE SERIES
CC5764	Waste: At the Source
CC5765	Waste: The Personal View
CC5766	Waste: The Global View
CC5767	Waste Management Big Book
	CLIMATE CHANGE SERIES
CC5769	Global Warming: Causes
CC5770	Global Warming: Effects
CC5771	Global Warming: Reduction
CC5772	Global Warming Big Book
	GLOBAL WATER SERIES
CC5773	Conservation: Fresh Water Resources
CC5774	Conservation: Ocean Water Resources
CC5775	Conservation: Waterway Habitat Resources
CC5776	Water Conservation Big Book
	CARBON FOOTPRINT SERIES
CC5778	Reducing Your Own Carbon Footprint
CC5779	Reducing Your School's Carbon Footprint
CC5780	Reducing Your Community's Carbon Footprint
CC5781	Carbon Footprint Big Book

SCIENCE - Software

ITEM #	TITLE
	SPACE AND BEYOND SERIES
CC7557	Solar System Grades 5-8
CC7558	Galaxies & the Universe Grades 5-8
CC7559	Space Travel & Technology Grades 5-8
CC7560	Space Big Box Grades 5-8
	HUMAN BODY SERIES
CC7549	Cells, Skeletal & Muscular Systems Grades 5-8
CC7550	Senses, Nervous & Respiratory Systems Grades 5-8
CC7551	Circulatory, Digestive & Reproductive Systems Grades 5-8
CC7552	Human Body Big Box Grades 5-8
	FORCE, MOTION & SIMPLE MACHINES SERIES
CC7553	Force Grades 3-8
CC7554	Motion Grades 3-8
CC7555	Simple Machines Grades 3-8
CC7556	Force, Motion & Simple Machines Big Box Grades 3-8

SCIENCE - Books

ITEM #	TITLE
	ECOLOGY & THE ENVIRONMENT SERIES
CC4500	Ecosystems
CC4501	Classification & Adaptation
CC4502	Cells
CC4503	Ecology & The Environment Big Book
	MATTER & ENERGY SERIES
CC4504	Properties of Matter
CC4505	Atoms, Molecules & Elements
CC4506	Energy
CC4507	The Nature of Matter Big Book
	FORCE & MOTION SERIES
CC4508	Force
CC4509	Motion
CC4510	Simple Machines
CC4511	Force, Motion & Simple Machines Big Book
	SPACE & BEYOND SERIES
CC4512	Solar System
CC4513	Galaxies & The Universe
CC4514	Travel & Technology
CC4515	Space Big Book
	HUMAN BODY SERIES
CC4516	Cells, Skeletal & Muscular Systems
CC4517	Senses, Nervous & Respiratory Systems
CC4518	Circulatory, Digestive & Reproductive Systems
CC4519	Human Body Big Book

LITERATURE KITS™ - Books

ITEM #	TITLE
	GRADES 1-2
CC2100	Curious George (H. A. Rey)
CC2101	Paper Bag Princess (Robert N. Munsch)
CC2102	Stone Soup (Marcia Brown)
CC2103	The Very Hungry Caterpillar (Eric Carle)
CC2104	Where the Wild Things Are (Maurice Sendak)
	GRADES 3-4
CC2300	Babe: The Gallant Pig (Dick King-Smith)
CC2301	Because of Winn-Dixie (Kate DiCamillo)
CC2302	The Tale of Despereaux (Kate DiCamillo)
CC2303	James and the Giant Peach (Roald Dahl)
CC2304	Ramona Quimby, Age 8 (Beverly Cleary)
CC2305	The Mouse and the Motorcycle (Beverly Cleary)
CC2306	Charlotte's Web (E.B. White)
CC2307	Owls in the Family (Farley Mowat)
CC2308	Sarah, Plain and Tall (Patricia MacLachlan)
CC2309	Matilda (Roald Dahl)
CC2310	Charlie & The Chocolate Factory (Roald Dahl)
CC2311	Frindle (Andrew Clements)
CC2312	M.C. Higgins, the Great (Virginia Hamilton)
CC2313	The Family Under The Bridge (N.S. Carlson)
CC2314	The Hundred Penny Box (Sharon Mathis)
CC2315	Cricket in Times Square (George Selden)
CC2316	Fantastic Mr Fox (Roald Dahl)
CC2317	The Hundred Dresses (Eleanor Estes)
	GRADES 5-6
CC2500	Hank the Cowdog (John Erickson)
CC2501	Bridge to Terabithia (Katherine Paterson)
CC2502	Bud, Not Buddy (Christopher Paul Curtis)
CC2503	The Egypt Game (Zilpha Keatley Snyder)
CC2504	The Great Gilly Hopkins (Katherine Paterson)
CC2505	Holes (Louis Sachar)
CC2506	Number the Stars (Lois Lowry)
CC2507	The Sign of the Beaver (E.G. Speare)
CC2508	The Whipping Boy (Sid Fleischman)
CC2509	Island of the Blue Dolphins (Scott O'Dell)
CC2510	Underground to Canada (Barbara Smucker)
CC2511	Loser (Jerry Spinelli)
CC2512	The Higher Power of Lucky (Susan Patron)
CC2513	Kira-Kira (Cynthia Kadohata)
CC2514	Dear Mr. Henshaw (Beverly Cleary)
CC2515	The Summer of the Swans (Betsy Byars)
CC2516	Shiloh (Phyllis Reynolds Naylor)
CC2517	A Single Shard (Linda Sue Park)
CC2518	Hoot (Carl Hiaasen)
CC2519	Hatchet (Gary Paulsen)
CC2520	The Giver (Lois Lowry)
CC2521	The Graveyard Book (Neil Gaiman)
CC2522	The View From Saturday (E.L. Konigsburg)
CC2523	Hattie Big Sky (Kirby Larson)
CC2524	When You Reach Me (Rebecca Stead)
CC2525	Criss Cross (Lynne Rae Perkins)
CC2526	A Year Down Yonder (Richard Peck)
CC2527	Maniac Magee (Jerry Spinelli)

LITERATURE KITS™ - Books

ITEM #	TITLE
CC2528	From the Mixed-Up Files of Mrs. Basil E. Frankweiler (E.L. Konigsburg)
CC2529	Sing Down the Moon (Scott O'Dell)
	GRADES 7-8
CC2700	Cheaper by the Dozen (Frank B. Gilbreth)
CC2701	The Miracle Worker (William Gibson)
CC2702	The Red Pony (John Steinbeck)
CC2703	Treasure Island (Robert Louis Stevenson)
CC2704	Romeo & Juliet (William Shakespeare)
CC2705	Crispin: The Cross of Lead (Avi)
CC2707	The Boy in the Striped Pajamas (John Boyne)
CC2708	The Westing Game (Ellen Raskin)
	GRADES 9-12
CC2001	To Kill A Mockingbird (Harper Lee)
CC2002	Angela's Ashes (Frank McCourt)
CC2003	The Grapes of Wrath (John Steinbeck)
CC2004	The Good Earth (Pearl S. Buck)
CC2005	The Road (Cormac McCarthy)
CC2006	The Old Man and the Sea (Ernest Hemingway)
CC2007	Lord of the Flies (William Golding)
CC2008	The Color Purple (Alice Walker)
CC2009	The Outsiders (S.E. Hinton)
CC2010	Hamlet (William Shakespeare)
CC2012	The Adventures of Huckleberry Finn (Mark Twain)
CC2013	Macbeth (William Shakespeare)

LANGUAGE ARTS - Software

ITEM #	TITLE
CC7115	Word Families - Short Vowels Grades PK-1
CC7113	Word Families - Long Vowels Grades PK-2
CC7114	Word Families - Vowels Big Box Grades PK-2
CC7100	High Frequency Sight Words Grades PK-2
CC7101	High Frequency Picture Words Grades PK-2
CC7102	Sight & Picture Words Big Box Grades PK-2
CC7104	How to Write a Paragraph Grades 3-8
CC7105	How to Write a Book Report Grades 3-8
CC7106	How to Write an Essay Grades 3-8
CC7107	Master Writing Big Box Grades 3-8
CC7108	Reading Comprehension Grades 5-8
CC7109	Literary Devices Grades 5-8
CC7110	Critical Thinking Grades 5-8
CC7111	Master Reading Big Box Grades 5-8

LANGUAGE ARTS - Books

ITEM #	TITLE
CC1110	Word Families - Short Vowels Grades K-1
CC1111	Word Families - Long Vowels Grades K-1
CC1112	Word Families - Vowels Big Book Grades K-1
CC1113	High Frequency Sight Words Grades K-1
CC1114	High Frequency Picture Words Grades K-1
CC1115	Sight & Picture Words Big Book Grades K-1
CC1100	How to Write a Paragraph Grades 5-8
CC1101	How to Write a Book Report Grades 5-8
CC1102	How to Write an Essay Grades 5-8
CC1103	Master Writing Big Book Grades 5-8
CC1116	Reading Comprehension Grades 5-8
CC1117	Literary Devices Grades 5-8
CC1118	Critical Thinking Grades 5-8
CC1119	Master Reading Big Book Grades 5-8
CC1106	Reading Response Forms: Grades 1-2
CC1107	Reading Response Forms: Grades 3-4
CC1108	Reading Response Forms: Grades 5-6
CC1109	Reading Response Forms Big Book: Grades 1-6

MATHEMATICS - Software

ITEM #	TITLE
	PRINCIPLES & STANDARDS OF MATH SERIES
CC7315	Grades PK-2 Five Strands of Math Big Box
CC7316	Grades 3-5 Five Strands of Math Big Box
CC7317	Grades 6-8 Five Strands of Math Big Box

MATHEMATICS - Books

ITEM #	TITLE
	TASK SHEETS
CC3100	Grades PK-2 Number & Operations Task Sheets
CC3101	Grades PK-2 Algebra Task Sheets
CC3102	Grades PK-2 Geometry Task Sheets
CC3103	Grades PK-2 Measurement Task Sheets
CC3104	Grades PK-2 Data Analysis & Probability Task Sheets
CC3105	Grades PK-2 Five Strands of Math Big Book Task Sheets
CC3106	Grades 3-5 Number & Operations Task Sheets
CC3107	Grades 3-5 Algebra Task Sheets
CC3108	Grades 3-5 Geometry Task Sheets
CC3109	Grades 3-5 Measurement Task Sheets
CC3110	Grades 3-5 Data Analysis & Probability Task Sheets
CC3111	Grades 3-5 Five Strands of Math Big Book Task Sheets
CC3112	Grades 6-8 Number & Operations Task Sheets
CC3113	Grades 6-8 Algebra Task Sheets
CC3114	Grades 6-8 Geometry Task Sheets
CC3115	Grades 6-8 Measurement Task Sheets
CC3116	Grades 6-8 Data Analysis & Probability Task Sheets
CC3117	Grades 6-8 Five Strands of Math Big Book Task Sheets
	DRILL SHEETS
CC3200	Grades PK-2 Number & Operations Drill Sheets
CC3201	Grades PK-2 Algebra Drill Sheets
CC3202	Grades PK-2 Geometry Drill Sheets
CC3203	Grades PK-2 Measurement Drill Sheets
CC3204	Grades PK-2 Data Analysis & Probability Drill Sheets
CC3205	Grades PK-2 Five Strands of Math Big Book Drill Sheets
CC3206	Grades 3-5 Number & Operations Drill Sheets
CC3207	Grades 3-5 Algebra Drill Sheets
CC3208	Grades 3-5 Geometry Drill Sheets
CC3209	Grades 3-5 Measurement Drill Sheets
CC3210	Grades 3-5 Data Analysis & Probability Drill Sheets
CC3211	Grades 3-5 Five Strands of Math Big Book Drill Sheets
CC3212	Grades 6-8 Number & Operations Drill Sheets
CC3213	Grades 6-8 Algebra Drill Sheets
CC3214	Grades 6-8 Geometry Drill Sheets
CC3215	Grades 6-8 Measurement Drill Sheets
CC3216	Grades 6-8 Data Analysis & Probability Drill Sheets
CC3217	Grades 6-8 Five Strands of Math Big Book Drill Sheets
	TASK & DRILL SHEETS
CC3300	Grades PK-2 Number & Operations Task & Drill Sheets
CC3301	Grades PK-2 Algebra Task & Drill Sheets
CC3302	Grades PK-2 Geometry Task & Drill Sheets
CC3303	Grades PK-2 Measurement Task & Drill Sheets
CC3304	Grades PK-2 Data Analysis & Probability Task & Drills
CC3306	Grades 3-5 Number & Operations Task & Drill Sheets
CC3307	Grades 3-5 Algebra Task & Drill Sheets
CC3308	Grades 3-5 Geometry Task & Drill Sheets
CC3309	Grades 3-5 Measurement Task & Drill Sheets
CC3310	Grades 3-5 Data Analysis & Probability Task & Drills
CC3312	Grades 6-8 Number & Operations Task & Drill Sheets
CC3313	Grades 6-8 Algebra Task & Drill Sheets
CC3314	Grades 6-8 Geometry Task & Drill Sheets
CC3315	Grades 6-8 Measurement Task & Drill Sheets
CC3316	Grades 6-8 Data Analysis & Probability Task & Drills